W9-BFE-355

Amazing Places

LIVE. LEARN. DISCOVER.

Parragon

Bath · New York · Singapore · Hong Kong · Cologne · Delhi · Melbourne

Amazing Places

Discover the **famous** wonders of our **world**

Author: Robert Hamilton
Consultant: Fiona Waters

First published by Parragon in 2009
Parragon
Queen Street House
4 Queen Street
Bath BA1 1HE, UK

ISBN 978-1-4075-6739-6
Printed in China

Contents

Fantastic features

The forces of nature have created some of the most spectacular sights on Earth. In this chapter, you will find out about mighty waterfalls and the world's longest river. You will learn about the coldest place on the planet, where a cup of coffee would freeze immediately, and about how a volcano formed a staircase fit for a giant!

Antarctica

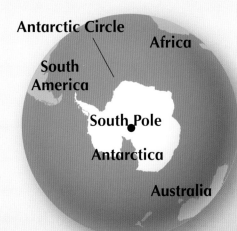

Antarctica is an ice desert, often called the "last great wilderness." No ship reached Antarctica until 1820, making it the last continent to be discovered. This is because the Southern Ocean surrounding Antarctica is so big and its stormy seas make it difficult to cross.

Naming Antarctica

People knew about the Arctic, the area around the North Pole, and guessed there must be land at the southern tip of the Earth, too. They called it the Antarctic—"the opposite of the Arctic." Unlike the Arctic, which is a frozen ocean, Antarctica is a continent—a vast area of land covered in ice.

Icebergs

The ice in Antarctica is over 2¹/₂ miles thick in places and it is always moving. Rivers of ice, called glaciers, flow toward the coast, traveling at a speed of 32 feet per year. When the ice reaches the ocean, huge blocks sometimes break off. These floating islands of ice are called icebergs.

Scientific research

Scientists from all over the world come to Antarctica to study changes in sea levels, weather, and climate. Although it is cold, visitors have to be careful not to get sunburned because the snow and ice reflect most of the Sun's rays.

Antarctic animals

About 98 percent of Antarctica is covered in ice. In summer, penguins and other birds gather on the small amount of bare rock to feed and to have their young. The area is safe from predators and there is plenty of food in the ocean.

Crabeater seal

DiscoveryFact™

Antarctica has the lowest temperature ever recorded, −128°F. A cup of coffee made with freshly boiled water would freeze immediately in that temperature.

Giant's Causeway

The extraordinary shape of these rocks in Northern Ireland amazed everyone when they were discovered 300 years ago. At first no one was sure if they were natural or artificial. The blocks of stone looked like a huge staircase or causeway, and people made up stories about a giant who built it to settle an argument with a rival across the sea.

Did you know?

- There are about 40,000 columns in the Causeway. Some of them are 39 feet high.

- There are similar rock formations on the Scottish island of Staffa. These supported the myth of the giant building a causeway across the sea.

This group of rocks is called the Wishing Chair.

Volcanic rocks

By 1800, scientists had proved that the columns in the Giant's Causeway were formed after a volcano erupted about 60 million years ago. When the lava cooled it cracked and broke up, forming a type of rock called basalt.

Giant's Causeway

North Sea

NORTHERN IRELAND

UNITED KINGDOM

Atlantic Ocean

Europe

The legend of Finn MacCool

Legend says that the giant Finn MacCool's rival, an even bigger giant called Benandonner, came across the sea on the causeway to fight him. Finn's wife wrapped Finn in a blanket and put him in a cradle. When Benandonner saw the "baby" and imagined how big its father must be, he turned and ran, ripping up the causeway as he went.

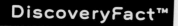

DiscoveryFact™

Many visitors sit in the Wishing Chair, a stone seat that is said to have been made for the giant Finn MacCool when he was a boy.

Crossing the sea

The Carrick-a-Rede Bridge is only a few minutes away from the Giant's Causeway. It links mainland Ireland to the tiny island of Carrick. The narrow rope bridge spans 65 feet and there is a 98-foot drop onto the rocks below.

The Matterhorn

The Matterhorn's pyramid shape has made it famous all over the world. It is in the Swiss Alps, near the border with Italy. The Matterhorn is 14,692 feet high—less than half the height of Mount Everest, the world's highest mountain. It isn't even the highest peak in the Alps, but its pyramid shape has drawn climbers to it for over 150 years.

North Sea

Europe

SWITZERLAND

•Matterhorn

DiscoveryFact™

The four sides of the Matterhorn face the four compass points—north, south, east, and west.

Did you know?

• A Matterhorn ride was one of the first attractions built when Disneyland opened in California in 1955. This rollercoaster ride is exactly 100 times smaller than the real mountain.

• The name "Matterhorn" comes from two German words, meaning "meadow peak."

Early mountaineers

In the 1800s, the Matterhorn inspired fear in climbers, and there were many failed attempts before the summit was reached. Many tried to go up the southern face, which looks easy from below but is really very difficult. A British climber called Edward Whymper thought that the northern face might be an easier route. He led a party of seven people to the top in 1865. Unfortunately, on the way down four of the climbers fell to their deaths.

The mountain today

Reaching the top of the Matterhorn is a lot easier today. A cable car takes climbers to the foot of the mountain, and there are ropes and ladders along the way to the peak. Climbers usually spend the night at a hut situated at 10,500 feet, then set out for the summit early the next morning. This gives them time to reach the summit and return to safety before the afternoon clouds or stormy weather arrives. Thousands climb the Matterhorn every summer, but there are many dangers. Rockfalls and avalanches kill several people every year.

The Nile River

The Nile is the world's longest river. It stretches about 4,000 miles from its source in central Africa to the north coast of Egypt, where it flows into the Mediterranean Sea. Before it reaches the sea, the Nile splits into several channels. This part of the river is called the Nile Delta.

Mediterranean Sea

Nile Delta

Cairo

River Nile

EGYPT

Red Sea

SUDAN

Khartoum

Blue Nile

White Nile

UGANDA

Lake Victoria

Traveling on the river

The ancient Egyptians made boats from reeds that grew beside the Nile. The wind carried them south; the river current carried them north. Today the Nile isn't as important as a means of transport but fishermen still use a flat-bottomed sailboat called a *felucca*.

Did you know?

- The source of the Nile is Lake Victoria, near the Equator.
- Some explorers have followed it even farther south, to rivers in Rwanda and Burundi.
- The Nile gets its name from the Greek word *"neilos,"* which means "river valley."

Ancient Egypt

The Ancient Egyptian civilization developed 5,000 years ago because of the Nile. The river flooded every year and left layers of rich silt on its banks. The Egyptians grew crops on this fertile land, and also fished in the river.

DiscoveryFact™

The Nile is formed from two main rivers, the Blue Nile and the White Nile. They meet at Khartoum, the capital of Sudan.

Yosemite

Yosemite is a vast wilderness, over 965 square miles of granite mountains, deep valleys, and spectacular waterfalls. About 2,000 species of animals and plants live there, including giant sequoia trees almost 3,000 years old.

Yosemite

UNITED STATES OF AMERICA

State of California

Pacific Ocean

El Capitan

Waterfalls

Yosemite is famous for its many waterfalls. Yosemite Falls are the highest in North America, at a height of 2,566 feet. The falls are best seen in the spring when the amount of water flowing over them increases as the winter snow melts.

Did you know?

- Half Dome is one of Yosemite's most famous mountains. Climbers have to be careful because the mountain is often hit by lightning.

- Tourists first arrived in 1855. There were 42 that year! Today Yosemite has about four million visitors a year.

Giant sequoias

The world's tallest, largest, and oldest trees grow in the western part of the United States. They are called giant sequoias. These trees are sometimes also called California redwoods because they grow in California and their wood is a reddish-brown color. Sequoias can grow to a height of 295 feet and can live for 3,000 years.

Yosemite Valley

DiscoveryFact™

In 1864, President Abraham Lincoln passed a law to protect Yosemite's natural beauty. It became a National Park in 1890.

Bears

The black bears that roam wild in Yosemite National Park have an amazing sense of smell. Campers have to be careful since they can seek out canned food, and will even eat soap!

The Grand Canyon

The Grand Canyon is the largest gorge on Earth. It is 5,250 feet deep, 277 miles long, and up to 18 miles wide. It was formed by the fast-flowing waters of the Colorado River, which have worn away the rock over millions of years. Wind, rain, and ice have also played a part in eroding the rock.

Layers of rock

New layers of rock are formed on the Earth's surface over millions of years, so looking at the sides of the canyon is like looking back in time. The layers at the bottom of the canyon are the oldest, formed almost two billion years ago. The top layers are quite young —just 250 million years old! Fossils buried in the layers of rock tell us about the animals that lived during different periods in the Earth's history.

Havasu Falls

Havasu Falls are famous for their blue-green color. The Havasupai tribe has lived in that area of the Grand Canyon for 800 years. The name of the tribe means "people of the bluish-green water."

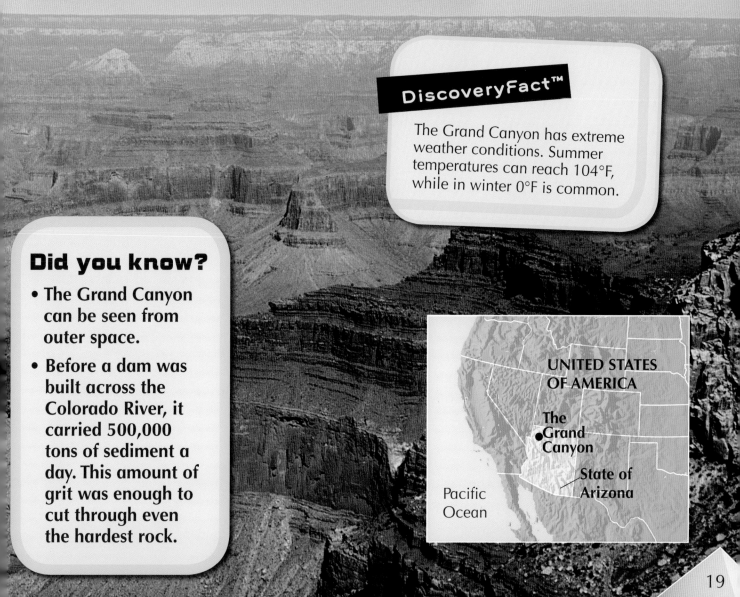

The Skywalk

The Skywalk, which opened in 2007, gives an amazing view of the Grand Canyon if you don't mind heights. It juts out 65 feet over the edge and has a floor made of glass. The Colorado River is 4,000 feet below.

DiscoveryFact™

The Grand Canyon has extreme weather conditions. Summer temperatures can reach 104°F, while in winter 0°F is common.

Did you know?

- The Grand Canyon can be seen from outer space.

- Before a dam was built across the Colorado River, it carried 500,000 tons of sediment a day. This amount of grit was enough to cut through even the hardest rock.

UNITED STATES OF AMERICA

The Grand Canyon

State of Arizona

Pacific Ocean

Waterfalls

Waterfalls form where a river flows over layers of hard and soft rocks lying next to each other. The water wears away the soft rock, leaving a shelf of hard rock above it. As the soft rock disappears, the waterfall gets bigger and steeper.

DiscoveryFact™

A daredevil acrobat named Blondin crossed Niagara Falls on a tightrope in 1859, carrying a friend on his back.

Victoria Falls

More water flows over Victoria Falls than any other waterfall in the world. These falls, which are situated in southern Africa, are 1 mile wide and 118 yards high. Over 1,100 tons of water per second drop into the Zambezi River below. The people who live there call it "the smoke that thunders" because in the rainy season the spray looks like smoke, which rises hundreds of yards into the air.

Did you know?

- Waterfalls move slowly upstream. This is because the hard rock that forms the shelf eventually breaks off. Niagara Falls is moving back by 3 feet per year.

Niagara Falls

Niagara Falls, which lie on the border between America and Canada, are among the most spectacular in the world. Water in the Niagara River has to flow around islands, so there are actually three separate waterfalls. They are called Horseshoe Falls, American Falls, and Bridal Veil Falls. At night most of Niagara's water doesn't flow over the falls. It's diverted into tunnels to turn turbines to make electricity.

Angel Falls

Angel Falls in Venezuela are the highest in the world. The water turns into a fine mist before it reaches the Churun River 1,070 yards below. Angel Falls are named after Jimmie Angel, an American adventurer who discovered them 70 years ago while searching for gold.

DiscoveryFact™

Victoria Falls were discovered by British explorer David Livingstone in 1855. He named them after Queen Victoria, who was the British monarch at the time.

Victoria Falls

Quick Quiz

Are these sentences TRUE or FALSE?
Place the correct sticker in the box.

1. About 98 percent of Antarctica is covered in ice.
2. The Matterhorn is higher than Mount Everest.
3. The Nile River is the longest river in the world.
4. Yosemite Falls are the highest in North America.
5. The Grand Canyon is 27 miles long.

Find the correct stickers to complete the pictures.

Egypt

Havasu Falls

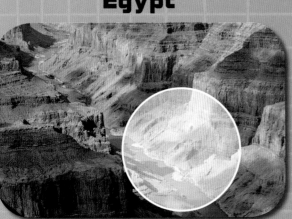

Grand Canyon

Yosemite Falls

ANSWERS: 1 – T, 2 – F, 3 – F, 4 – T, 5 – F

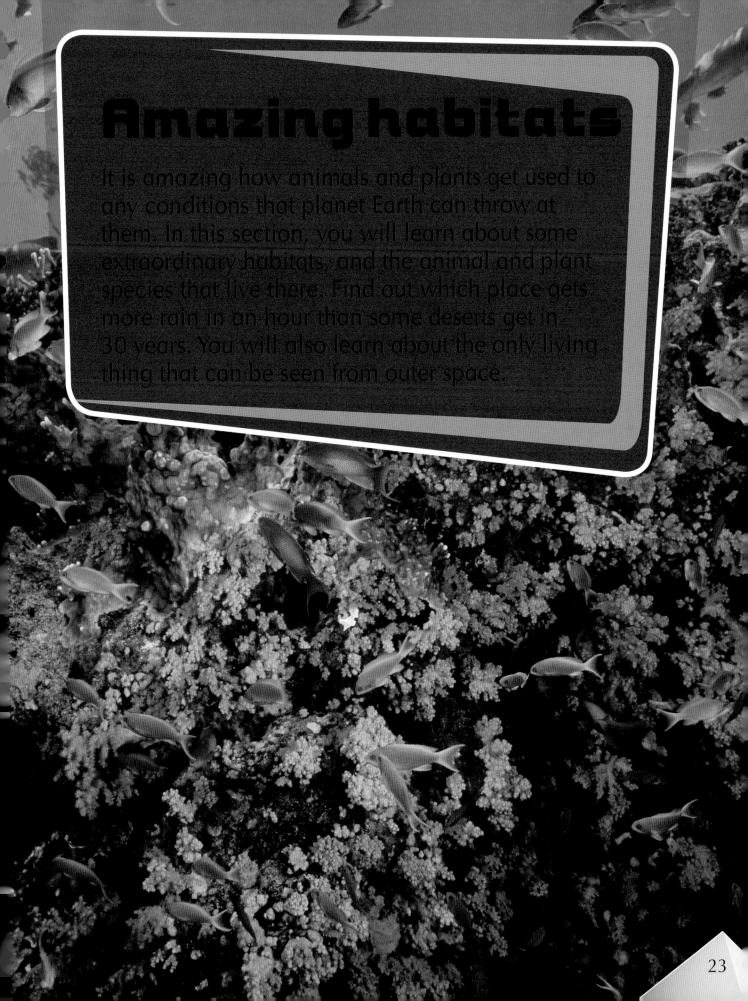

Amazing habitats

It is amazing how animals and plants get used to any conditions that planet Earth can throw at them. In this section, you will learn about some extraordinary habitats, and the animal and plant species that live there. Find out which place gets more rain in an hour than some deserts get in 30 years. You will also learn about the only living thing that can be seen from outer space.

The Sahara

The Sahara is the world's largest desert, covering most of northern Africa. It is one of the hottest places on Earth, but it is the dryness of the place that makes it a desert, not its heat. Only about 2½ inches of rain fall per year on average. Most of the desert is rocky, although there are many high sand dunes.

Pools of water

An oasis is an area in the desert where water trapped deep under the ground comes to the surface. This allows plants and trees to grow and provides small patches of green among the desert's rocks and sand. Oases are also vital water sources for people who live in the desert. People can settle here and grow crops such as date palms.

Western Sahara
Algeria
Libya
Egypt
Mauritania
SAHARA DESERT
Mali
Niger
Chad
Sudan
Ethiopia
Africa

Camels—ships of the desert

Camels are used to carry merchandise across the Sahara, like ships carry merchandise across the sea. They have adapted well to life in the desert. Their humps contain fat, which can provide them with both food and water. Their wide feet allow them to walk on soft sand and they have thick soles to withstand heat from the ground. They can also close their nostrils against the sand and dust of the desert.

DiscoveryFact™

The world's highest recorded temperature in the shade was in the Sahara on September 13, 1922—a sizzling 136°F at Al Aziziyan in Libya.

Desert animals

Snakes, gerbils, lizards, and scorpions all live in the desert. These small animals may hide from the hot sun in the shade of the rocks or dig burrows in the sand. The fat-tailed scorpion hides away under rocks or logs. It grows up to 4 inches long and is one of the most deadly scorpions in the world.

Madagascar

Madagascar is a large island off the southeastern coast of Africa. It was cut off from the mainland more than 150 million years ago. Since then the animals and plants on Madagascar have evolved without influence from the rest of the world. Now there are thousands of species on the island that are found nowhere else on Earth.

Changing colors!

Many species of chameleons live on the island of Madagascar. Chameleons are known for their ability to change color, and many people believe that chameleons change color to match their surroundings. In fact, their skin changes in response to temperature, light, and mood.

Madagascan frogs

The tomato frog is just one of many strange kinds of frogs that live in the shallow pools and swamps in the lowlands of Madagascar. The male frog is smaller and is not as brightly colored as the female. The tomato frog releases a sticky glue-like liquid through its skin that protects it against snakes and other creatures.

Did you know?

- The rosy periwinkle, a plant which lives only in Madagascar, is used by doctors to treat cancer.

- Frogs are the only amphibians found on Madagascar—there are no toads, newts, or salamanders.

Many different kinds of baobab trees grow on Madagascar.

Africa

Indian Ocean

MADAGASCAR

Lemurs

Madagascar is the only place on Earth where lemurs can be found. Lemurs look a little like monkeys since they have grasping fingers and toes and forward-looking eyes. But there are differences because lemurs have large, round eyes and a snout that looks as though it could belong to a cat or dog!

27

The Great Barrier Reef

The Great Barrier Reef is the largest living thing in the world. It is formed from millions of tiny animals called coral polyps, which have joined together to form a reef that runs for 1,240 miles along the northeast coast of Australia.

Indian Ocean

The Great Barrier Reef

AUSTRALIA

Indian Ocean

A clown fish on the reef

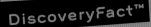

DiscoveryFact™

The Great Barrier Reef is the only living thing that can be seen from space.

What is coral?

Coral polyps are tiny sea creatures with limestone shells. Over the centuries these shells build up to form coral reefs. Although corals are animals, they need sunlight to grow, like plants. That's because the corals contain thousands of algae, tiny plants. Like all plants, the algae use sunlight to make food, both for themselves and for the coral. It is the algae that give the coral its bright colors.

Thousands of fish

Coral reefs provide shelter and food for hundreds of thousands of living things. The blue chromis above are one of more than 1,500 species of fish that live on the reef.

Did you know?

- The reef is under threat from rising sea temperatures. The warm water stops the algae inside the coral from producing food. The algae become poisonous, so the coral spits them out. Without the algae to provide food, the coral dies and turns white.

Turtles

Six species of sea turtles are found in the waters around the Great Barrier Reef. Turtles, like this green turtle, spend most of their lives in the ocean, feeding on sea grasses and corals, though females come ashore to lay their eggs.

Giant clams

The shell of a giant clam can measure up to 47 inches in length and weigh nearly 500 pounds. Once a clam fastens itself to a spot on a reef, it stays there for the rest of its life.

The Rocky Mountains

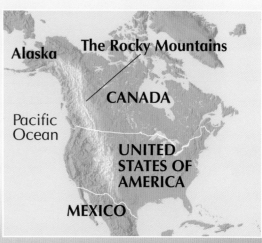

Alaska
The Rocky Mountains

CANADA

Pacific
Ocean

UNITED
STATES OF
AMERICA

MEXICO

The Rocky Mountains form the backbone of North America. They stretch from Alaska, through the western parts of Canada and the U.S., coming to an end in New Mexico. The tallest mountains are over 157,000 feet high with jagged, rocky peaks and slopes covered in snow and glaciers. Others have gentle slopes with rounded tops.

Mountain animals

Deer, elk, and coyotes are some of the larger mammals found in the Rockies, but mountain lions are the most magnificent. The mountain lion, sometimes known as the cougar, is a solitary animal that hunts by day and night. It will eat just about anything—from a grasshopper to a deer.

Keeping warm

Winters in the Rocky Mountains can be bitterly cold with deep snow and high winds. Black, brown, and grizzly bears are protected in these cold winter months by their thick fur coats and layers of fat. In summer and early fall they eat plenty of fruits, nuts, and berries as well as insects, roots, and small mammals in order to build up their store of fat for the winter.

Did you know?

- Early explorers gave the mountains their name because of the rugged landscape.
- The highest peak in the Rocky Mountains is Mount Elbert in Colorado, at 14,435 feet.

Mountain goat

The mountain goat is a sturdy animal, with a coat made of thick, coarse hair to protect it from the cold and fierce winds. Its hooves have a hard outside rim and cushioned inner pad, which help it to leap over rocks.

The Everglades

The Everglades is a vast wilderness of swamp and marshland in southern Florida. The shallow waters and 10,000 islands are home to some rare and endangered species, such as the enormous manatee.

UNITED STATES OF AMERICA

Florida

Atlantic Ocean

Gulf of Mexico

The ● Everglades

What grows in the Everglades?

A lot of the land in the Everglades is covered with sawgrass, which grows to a height of 9 to 15 feet. Sawgrass is very sharp. It has tiny teeth along the edges of the blades that can cut flesh. There are many hummocks, or small, fertile, raised areas, on which palms, pine trees, cypresses, and other trees and shrubs can grow.

Roots

Wherever the swamps border the coastline, the trees have adapted to live in salt water. Their roots stick out of the mud to help the plants take in the oxygen they need from the air.

DiscoveryFact™

There are four species of poisonous snakes in the Everglades. These are the cottonmouth, the diamondback rattlesnake, the dusky pygmy rattlesnake, and the coral snake.

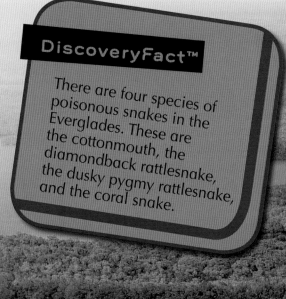

The gentle manatee

The Everglades are home to the manatee in the winter months. Manatees are marine mammals and they are forced to come to the surface to breathe air. Like seals, they have blubber under their thick skin to protect them from the cold and they can weigh up to 990 pounds. The manatee feeds on the sea grasses and plants that grow in the shallow water of the Everglades.

Alligators

The alligator is one of over 50 species of reptiles that live in the Everglades. Alligators are fierce predators, but they also play an important part in the survival of many species. During the dry winter months, from December to April, alligators dig large holes where water collects. This helps insects, turtles, fish, and wading birds to survive until the rainy season arrives—but they have to try to avoid being eaten by the alligators!

The Amazon rain forest

The Amazon rain forest is the largest in the world, covering over two million square miles, an area about the size of Australia. It is home to more plant and animal species than any other habitat on Earth, and new ones are being discovered every year.

The Amazon River

The Amazon River flows over 4,000 miles from the Andes Mountains in Peru to the Atlantic Ocean. The Amazon and the 1,000 smaller rivers that feed into it holds 20 percent of all the world's fresh water. Over 3,000 gallons of water flow from the Amazon into the Atlantic Ocean every second. The seawater is diluted so much by the freshwater from the Amazon that it is still only slightly salty 90 miles out into the ocean.

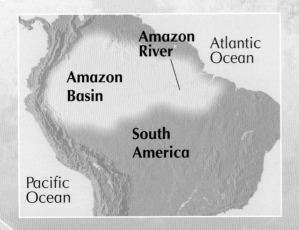

Amazon River
Atlantic Ocean
Amazon Basin
South America
Pacific Ocean

The forest floor

Jaguars are the Amazon rain forest's fiercest hunters. Their spotted coat helps to keep them hidden in the undergrowth as they stalk their prey, which includes cattle and pigs. The rain forest floor is dark because most of the sunlight is absorbed in the treetops 130 feet above. The branches spread out to form a large leafy blanket called a canopy, where most of the rain forest's plants and animals live.

Colorful birds

Macaws are one of 1,500 bird species that live in the rain forest. These brightly colored members of the parrot family gather in large numbers on the clay cliffs of the Amazon River. Here they feed on minerals that are thought to protect them from any poisons in the seeds they eat. Macaws use their powerful hooked beaks to crack open the shells that surround the seeds.

DiscoveryFact™

More than 2 inches of rain can fall in an hour in the Amazon rain forest. The rain forest canopy is so thick that after heavy rainfall it can take 10 minutes for the first drops of water to reach the forest floor.

The anaconda

The anaconda is the world's largest snake, able to grow to over 32 feet long. It is an excellent swimmer and climber and is usually found along the river's edge, waiting for an unlucky creature to come to the bank to drink. This powerful snake will attack animals as large as deer and goats. It kills its prey by coiling around it and squeezing tightly, or by dragging it underwater and drowning it.

Quick Quiz

Are these sentences TRUE or FALSE?
Place the correct sticker in the box.

1. The Sahara is the world's smallest desert.
2. Frogs are the only amphibians found on Madagascar.
3. The Great Barrier Reef can be seen from space.
4. There are no poisonous snakes in the Everglades.
5. The Amazon rain forest has an area the size of Australia.

Find the correct stickers to complete the pictures.

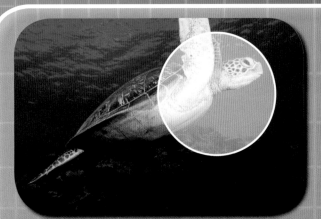

Great Barrier Reef

Rocky Mountains

Everglades

Amazon rain forest

ANSWERS: 1 – F, 2 – T, 3 – T, 4 – F, 5 – T

Ancient wonders

Some of the world's most amazing structures were built long before the wheel was invented, never mind cranes and trucks! In this section, you will discover many other wonders of the ancient world, such as the stadium where Roman gladiators and wild beasts fought to the death, and cave paintings that are 16,000 years old.

Stonehenge

Stonehenge, in Wiltshire, England, is the most famous stone circle in the world. No one is quite sure how or why it was built—some people think it might have been a giant calendar.

Atlantic Ocean

UNITED KINGDOM

South Wales

●Stonehenge

Europe

lintel

sarsen stone

The monument

Archaeologists think Stonehenge was built in three phases over a period of time beginning in about 3000 B.C. The original part of the structure was a large circular ditch and bank called a henge. The famous "standing stones" were added over a period of almost 200 years. The 82 bluestones were brought to the site first. Many people believe that they were dragged and carried on rafts from quarries in South Wales, over 200 miles away. The largest stones, called sarsen stones, were the final addition. These were placed in pairs, each pair supporting a massive horizontal lintel.

Did you know?

- The tallest archway at Stonehenge stands 25 feet high.

- The bluestones are so called because they turn blue when they are wet.

Avebury Henge

At Avebury, which is about 18 miles away from Stonehenge, you can clearly see the ancient henge. The enormous circular ditch is more than 32 feet deep and has a circumference of more than half a mile.

Religion

Thousands of people gather at Stonehenge every year on the Summer Solstice to watch the sunrise and celebrate the cycle of life, death, and rebirth. Most people think that Stonehenge was once a very important place for religious meetings. Some archaeologists suggest that it was used to look at the movements of the Sun and Moon.

Lascaux Caves

UK

Europe

Atlantic Ocean

FRANCE

• Lascaux

In 1940, four teenage boys followed their dog into some caves at Lascaux in southwestern France. On the walls inside they found some of the oldest paintings in the world, believed to date back at least 15,000 years.

Inside the caves

Prehistoric hunters painted the walls of the Lascaux caves. There are hundreds of paintings, many of which are deep inside the caves and difficult to reach. They show several different animals including horses, stags, cattle, bison, and even a few birds. Strangely, there are no images of reindeer, even though they were the main animals hunted by the cavemen. The pictures are in shades of red, brown, yellow, and black.

DiscoveryFact™

The paint used in the caves was made from ground-up earth and rocks, probably mixed with animal blood and fat.

The dead man

There is only one picture of a person in the caves. The man is lying dead or dying in front of a wounded bison. It looks as though it is a painting of a hunting accident.

Why were they painted?

No one is quite sure why the hunters painted animals on the walls of caves. Some experts think that the paintings were a form of magic to help the hunters catch their prey. Another idea is that the cavemen believed that they had to paint the animals on the wall to replace those that had been killed.

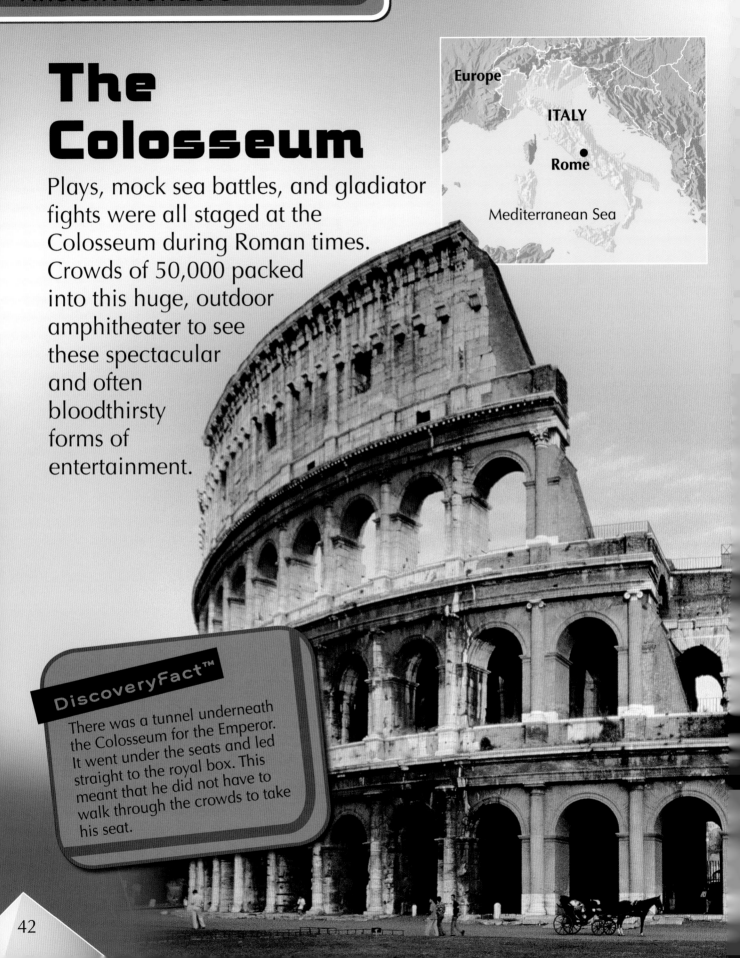

The Colosseum

Plays, mock sea battles, and gladiator fights were all staged at the Colosseum during Roman times. Crowds of 50,000 packed into this huge, outdoor amphitheater to see these spectacular and often bloodthirsty forms of entertainment.

Europe

ITALY

Rome

Mediterranean Sea

DiscoveryFact™

There was a tunnel underneath the Colosseum for the Emperor. It went under the seats and led straight to the royal box. This meant that he did not have to walk through the crowds to take his seat.

Gladiators

Most gladiators were slaves or criminals. They were brought to Rome from all parts of the empire and trained in special schools so that they could entertain the Colosseum crowds with bloody combat games. Gladiators were made to fight each other, or against wild beasts such as lions, tigers, and crocodiles.

The Colosseum was completed in 80 A.D. It is made from stone and concrete.

The arena

In the center of the Colosseum there was a flat area called the arena. This is where all the action took place. Underneath the arena was a series of underground tunnels and rooms, which we can see today because the arena floor has not survived. Fighters waited here, but it was also where animals were kept for the wild beast games.

The Acropolis

The Acropolis was built 2,500 years ago to protect the citizens of Athens from invaders. It stands on a hill overlooking the city, which was the safest place for the people and their sacred temples.

Europe

Black Sea

GREECE

Athens ●

Mediterranean Sea

The Parthenon

The Parthenon

The Parthenon is the most famous of all the buildings on the Acropolis. It is a great temple built by the Ancient Athenians to honor Athena, the goddess of wisdom and war. The temple was built about 2,500 years ago by the command of the leader Pericles of Athens. The Ancient Greeks believed that Athena could protect their city and so they loved and worshiped her.

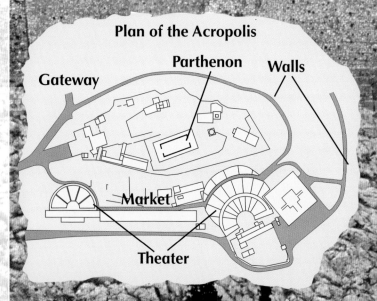

Plan of the Acropolis

Parthenon

Walls

Gateway

Market

Theater

The theater

The theater of Herodes Atticus was one of two outdoor theaters on the Acropolis. A large semicircle of seats was cut into a hillside with a flat stage area at the bottom. Theaters were so well designed that you could hear the actors speaking on stage in the top row of seats. Those in the back rows needed help to see what was happening on stage and so actors wore masks to show who they were playing.

DiscoveryFact™

The Parthenon looks almost white today but it was originally brightly painted and decorated with many sculptures.

Greek columns

The tall, slim columns of the Parthenon and other temples were decorated with grooves, which were carved in them from top to bottom. Although the columns look perfectly straight, they actually have a bulge in the middle. This is because tall straight columns look narrower in the middle. The Greek architects did not want their columns to appear uneven and so they made them fatter in the middle.

45

The Pyramids at Giza

The pyramids are the most famous monuments of Ancient Egypt. The largest pyramid of all is the Great Pyramid at Giza, just outside the modern city of Cairo. It was built for King Khufu in about 2528 B.C. There are two other large pyramids at Giza, which belong to Khufu's son, Khafre, and his grandson, Menkaure.

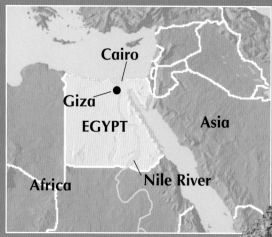

Cairo

Giza

EGYPT

Asia

Africa

Nile River

Building blocks

Khufu's Great Pyramid was built from over two million large blocks of stone cut from nearby quarries. These are believed to weigh about $2\frac{1}{2}$ tons—although the stones at the base of the pyramid are even heavier. When it was originally built, the pyramid was covered with limestone blocks so that its outer surface was smooth and white.

The Sphinx

The Sphinx at Giza was carved about 4,500 years ago for the pharaoh Khafre. It guarded the way to his pyramid. The Sphinx is carved from limestone and has the head of the king combined with the body of a lion, making a link between the strength of the lion and the pharaoh's great power.

DiscoveryFact™

Although the pyramids are believed to have been the burial places of the pharaohs, no one has ever found the mummy of a pharaoh in a pyramid.

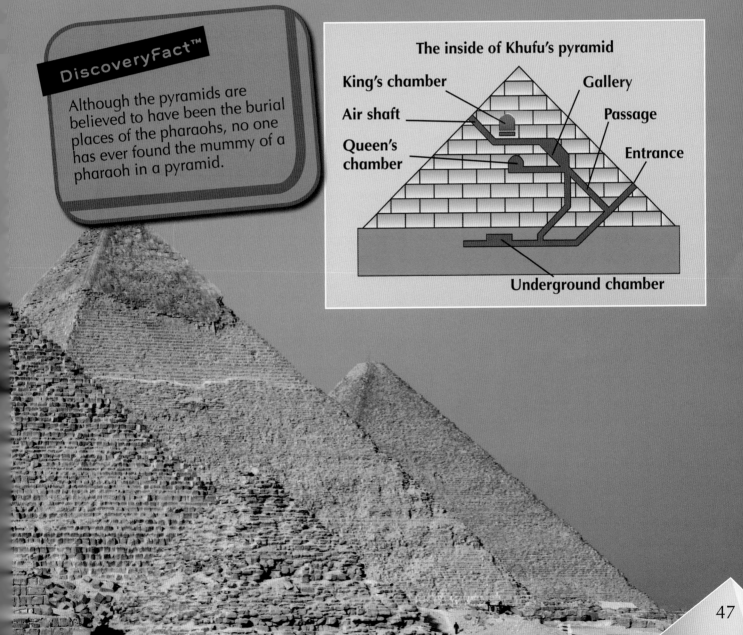

The inside of Khufu's pyramid

King's chamber

Gallery

Air shaft

Passage

Queen's chamber

Entrance

Underground chamber

Teotihuacán

Fifteen hundred years ago Teotihuacán in Mexico was the greatest city in North or South America, and one of the largest in the world. This ancient civilization, with a population of over 100,000, mysteriously died out around the 700s, leaving behind a number of amazing pyramid temples.

North America

Atlantic Ocean

MEXICO

Pacific Ocean

●Teotihuacán

South America

The Pyramid of the Sun is about 700 feet long and just over 200 feet high.

Quetzalcoatl's temple

The temple of the ancient god Quetzalcoatl is inside the Citadel, a large open space at the center of Teotihuacán. When archaeologists uncovered the temple in about 1920 much of it had collapsed. One side has survived and huge serpents' heads made of stone, each of which weighs over 4 tons, stick out of the wall.

Sacrifices

Human sacrifices were made as gifts to the gods. Sacrifices took place on top of the temple when the priests cut out the hearts of their victims. Many groups of human skeletons have been found at Teotihuacán. Those discovered at the Temple of Quetzalcoatl seemed to be warriors, judging by their clothing. Several wore necklaces of shells carved to look like jaws with teeth.

Did you know?

- The pyramids look very plain today but when they were built they would have been decorated with colorful paintings.

- The base of the Pyramid of the Sun at Teotihuacán is as large as the base of the Great Pyramid at Giza in Egypt.

DiscoveryFact™

Teotihuacán was built around the Avenue of the Dead, the city's main street, which runs in a north–south direction. The people believed that north represented death and the underworld, so tombs were usually built there.

Quick Quiz

Are these sentences TRUE or FALSE?
Place the correct sticker in the box.

1. [ ] Stonehenge is found in London, England.
2. [ ] The Lascaux caves are found in France.
3. [ ] The Acropolis was built 250 years ago.
4. [ ] The Romans built the pyramids.
5. [ ] The ruins of Teotihuacán are found in China.

Find the correct stickers to complete the pictures.

Stonehenge

Lascaux caves

The Colosseum

Teotihuácan

ANSWERS: 1 –F, 2 –T, 3 –F, 4 – F, 5 –F

Spectacular cities

In the past 200 years the Earth's population has grown from 1 billion to over 6 billion. All of the world's cities have expanded enormously during that period. In this section, we look at amazing cities, both ancient and modern. Discover the city that holds the world's biggest street party. Find out which city has canals instead of roads and which one sets the clocks for all the others.

London

A famous writer named Samuel Johnson once said, "When a man is tired of London, he is tired of life." He meant that there is so much to see and do in the city, it is impossible to be bored. Johnson wrote that over 200 years ago, and today London has even more places of interest.

City on the Thames

London is centered on the River Thames. Some of the city's best-known buildings are found along its banks. The Tower of London is an ancient fortress, which was founded by William the Conqueror almost 1,000 years ago. Over the centuries the Tower has been used as a palace, a prison, and an armory. Today many people visit the Tower to see the priceless Crown Jewels, which have been kept in the tower since 1303.

Changing the Guard

Buckingham Palace is the home of the Queen and it is protected by the Household Guard, who usually wear red jackets and tall hats called bearskins. The Changing of the Guard is a colorful ceremony that takes place in front of the Palace on most mornings.

Tower of London

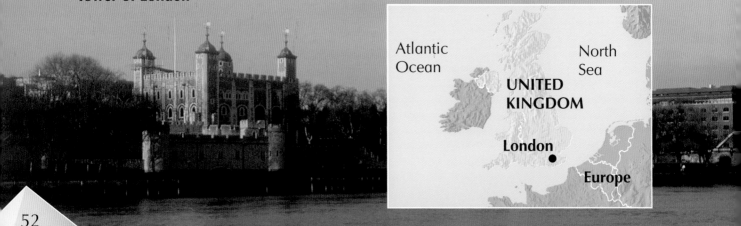

Atlantic Ocean

North Sea

UNITED KINGDOM

London

Europe

London Eye

The London Eye, at 443 feet high, is one of the world's largest observation wheels. During the 30-minute round trip passengers can see up to 25 miles.

Big Ben

Big Ben is the name of the huge 14-ton bell inside the clock tower of the Houses of Parliament. It is named after Sir Benjamin Hall, the man in charge of the building when the bell was installed in 1858.

Tower Bridge was built in 1894.

DiscoveryFact™

13 million people live in London and its suburbs, making it Europe's largest city.

Paris

Paris is famous for food and fashion. It is also celebrated for its museums and galleries, and is often described as the most romantic city in the world.

The Seine

Paris is divided in two by the Seine River. The south side of the river is called the Left Bank and the north side is called the Right Bank. The Left Bank was traditionally the home of artists, writers, and philosophers. There are two natural islands in the middle of the river, the Ile de la Cité and the Ile St. Louis.

The Louvre

The Louvre was a royal palace before becoming a museum in 1793. Visitors enter the world-famous building through a 65-foot-high glass pyramid, which was added in 1993.

The Arc de Triomphe

The Arc de Triomphe was built in 1836 to honor the great battles won by Napoleon Bonaparte, the army general who became Emperor of France in 1804. Parisians still gather at the 164-foot-high arch when there is a French victory to celebrate.

Did you know?

- Notre Dame cathedral is regarded as the exact center of Paris. Distances on road signs are worked out from this spot.

- Paris is the birthplace of the movies. The first film was shown there in 1895.

- About one fifth of France's entire population live in Paris and its suburbs.

Paris's most famous tourist attraction is the 1,000-foot-high Eiffel Tower.

Notre Dame

Notre Dame cathedral stands on Ile de la Cité, the larger of the two islands in the middle of the Seine River. The cathedral, whose name means "Our Lady," took almost 200 years to build and was completed in 1345.

Venice

Venice has canals instead of roads, boats instead of cars. People travel on waterbuses, catch water taxis, or rent rowboats called gondolas. Even ambulances and fire engines have to use the waterways!

City of islands

Venice was founded 1,500 years ago when people settled on a group of small islands, driving wooden posts into the mudbanks and building their houses on top of these. This magical city is made up of 118 islands and is famous for its art treasures and magnificent buildings.

The Grand Canal

The Grand Canal is Venice's Main Street. It is 2 miles long and winds through the center of the city. Some of the buildings that line the canal date back to the 1100s. The Rialto Bridge is the oldest and most famous of the three bridges spanning the Grand Canal.

Europe

Venice

ITALY

Mediterranean Sea

Gondolas

Those who want a relaxed canal journey travel by gondola, a rowboat steered with a single oar by a gondolier.

Magical carnival

The Venice Carnival, with its elaborate costumes, is the highlight of the city's year. St. Mark's Square and the theaters burst into life with musical, theatrical, and acrobatic performances. The carnival is 800 years old, one of the most celebrated and fascinating events in Europe.

DiscoveryFact™

Venice has over 400 bridges, more than any other city in the world.

Rio de Janeiro

If you like parties, Rio de Janeiro in Brazil has the biggest of them all. It is called Carnival and takes place in February or March each year.

Carnival

The highlight of the Carnival is the colorful parade. Thousands of people, dressed in elaborate costumes which are often decorated with feathers, sequins, mirrors, or metal, dance to samba music. As soon as the party is over, many people start making costumes for the next Carnival.

Did you know?

- Rio de Janeiro means "River of January." The Portuguese explorers who named it arrived in January 1502.

- Rio de Janeiro was the capital of Brazil until 1960, when a new city, Brasilia, was given that honor.

- Carnival takes place just before Lent, when Christians often give up certain foods. The people want to have a good time first.

DiscoveryFact™

On New Year's Eve people throw gifts into the sea. They hope the Sea Goddess will bring them luck for the next year.

Atlantic Ocean

South America

BRAZIL

Rio de Janeiro

Pacific Ocean

Rio's Beaches

Rio has a 30-mile coastline and many beautiful beaches. The most famous of these is Copacabana. Soccer, volleyball, and surfing are popular pastimes on this 2½ mile stretch of white sand.

Rio's famous statue

Rio's most famous landmark is the statue of Jesus Christ, which overlooks the city from the top of Corcovado mountain. The 130-foot-high statue, called Christ the Redeemer, was built in 1931. The local people like to think the statue's outstretched arms are embracing and protecting the city.

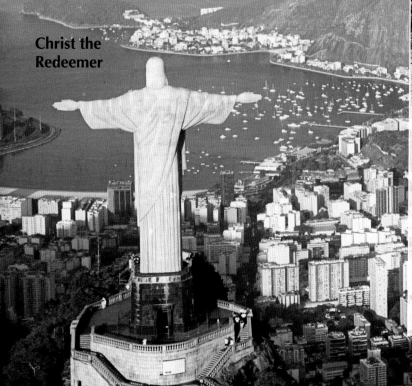

Christ the Redeemer

The Maracana

The Maracana is one of the largest and most famous stadiums in the world. Over 180,000 people once watched a soccer match there. Now it is an all-seater stadium holding 95,000. Pop concerts take place there as well as sports events.

Sydney

Sydney today is a beautiful, modern city, but 200 years ago people who committed crimes in England were sent there as a punishment. The first convict ships arrived in 1788, and the British flag was raised in Sydney Harbor. Native Aborigines had lived in Australia for thousands of years, and now had to share their homeland.

Sydney Harbor

Sydney grew to become the largest city in Australia, though Canberra was chosen as the capital. The famous harbor splits Sydney in two. The two sides were joined in 1932 when the Sydney Harbor Brige was opened. The many beaches are popular almost all year round as Sydney enjoys a warm, sunny climate.

Bondi Beach

Australians and tourists flock to Bondi Beach for the sun and surf. Surfing arrived in the city in 1914, when a visitor from Hawaii amazed local people with his ability to ride the waves on a board. Since then surfing has become a very popular sport throughout Australia.

The architect said that the roof design of the Sydney Opera House was inspired by peeling an orange.

Top Facts

- The world's first lifeguards began work on Bondi Beach in 1906.

- Australians call Sydney Harbor Bridge "The Coathanger" because of its shape. Today there is a tunnel under the harbor, so the bridge is not so important for transport.

- On March 18, 2007, over 200,000 people walked across Sydney Harbor Bridge to celebrate its 75th birthday.

The Opera House

Sydney Opera House is one of the world's most famous buildings. There are five separate theaters inside the building, where people can see operas, plays, and ballets and hear concerts. The largest building is the concert hall (above).

Pacific Ocean

AUSTRALIA

Sydney

Indian Ocean

DiscoveryFact™

An English explorer called Matthew Flinders suggested naming the country Australia, from the Latin word meaning "southern." Before then it was called New Holland.

New York City

New York has one of the most recognizable skylines of any city. The world's first skyscraper was built there in 1902. The Statue of Liberty in New York harbor is a symbol of the freedom and opportunity that the U.S. values so highly.

Manhattan

New York was originally ruled by the Dutch and called New Amsterdam. In 1664 the British took over and it was renamed New York. Today five large boroughs make up New York City, but it is the island of Manhattan that attracts most tourists. Manhattan has many famous landmarks, museums, and shops. Wall Street in Manhattan is the financial center of the U.S..

The Statue of Liberty

The Statue of Liberty was built in 1886. It was a gift from France to mark the 100th anniversary of American independence.

New York State

New York City

UNITED STATES OF AMERICA

Pacific Ocean

Atlantic Ocean

Central Park

Twenty million people a year visit Central Park, a 1.3-square-mile park that contains a lake, a zoo, and a museum as well as many sporting facilities, such as an outdoor ice rink in winter.

DiscoveryFact™

New York City is famous for its yellow taxi cabs. There are 12,000 of them!

Times Square

Times Square is the center of New York's entertainment district. The Broadway theaters nearby are famous the world over, and the Square's electric billboards are themselves a popular tourist attraction.

Did you know?

- New York is home to Macy's, the world's largest department store. It was just a corner store when it was founded in 1857.

- New York is called the "Big Apple." It was given its nickname by jazz musicians in the 1930s.

Quick Quiz

Are these sentences TRUE or FALSE?
Place the correct sticker in the box.

1. London is Europe's largest city.
2. The Eiffel Tower stands at 1,000-feet-high.
3. Rio de Janeiro means "River of December."
4. The capital of Australia is Sydney.
5. New York is home to the worlds largest department store.

Find the correct stickers to complete the pictures.

London

Paris

Rio de Janeiro

New York

ANSWERS: 1 – T, 2 – T, 3 – F, 4 – F, 5 – T

Astonishing structures

Strong feelings and deep beliefs have been the inspiration behind some of the world's most spectacular buildings. In this section, we look at how religion, friendship, grief, and fear have led to some amazing structures being built. Find out about the people so afraid of invaders that they built a 3,700-mile wall to keep them out. Learn about the emperor who was so upset when his wife died that he ordered 2,000 people to spend 20 years building her a magnificent tomb!

The Eiffel Tower

When it was built in 1889, the Eiffel Tower was the tallest structure in the world. The tower weighs about 7,200 tons and is made from over 18,000 pieces of iron.

Why was the tower built?

The Eiffel Tower was built for the 1889 Universal Exposition in Paris. The Exposition, or exhibition, was arranged to celebrate the 100th anniversary of the French Revolution. The French government wanted the rest of the world to marvel at their great work made from iron, but many Parisians were afraid that it would collapse on the city. Alexandre Gustave Eiffel, the engineer who was building the tower, continued his work, confident that it would be safe.

Building the tower

It took 250 men just over two years to build the Eiffel Tower.

Alexandre Gustave Eiffel

Eiffel was one of France's greatest engineers, and built many bridges. Eiffel's experience of working with metal bridges helped him calculate how the tower should be constructed so that it did not collapse or blow around in the wind. Eiffel also used his understanding of metals to design the framework for the Statue of Liberty.

Visiting the tower

There are 1,665 steps to the top of the tower. Today you can only climb as high as the second floor and then you have to take an elevator the rest of the way up. The tower welcomes six million tourists each year. More than 200 million people have visited it since it was built.

Red Square

Red Square, in the center of Moscow, is home to some of the most spectacular and important buildings in Russia.

Arctic Ocean

Moscow

RUSSIA

Asia

St. Basil's Cathedral

St. Basil's Cathedral

With its brightly colored onion-shaped domes, St. Basil's Cathedral is one of the most famous monuments in Russia. The cathedral was built in the 1550s and commemorates Russia's victory over its great enemy, the Khanate of Kazan. The Russian czar, or ruler, at this time was Ivan the Terrible and it is said that Ivan blinded the architects of the cathedral so that they could never build anything better.

The domes

St. Basil's Cathedral is decorated with eight colorful domes.

The Kremlin

The city of Moscow was originally built within a medieval fortress called the Kremlin. It was protected from invaders by a great wall, more than 6,500 feet long. Inside the walls are palaces, cathedrals, churches, and government buildings.

State Historical Museum

On the north side of Red Square is the State Historical Museum. It was built at the end of the 1800s and opened in 1894. The museum contains many millions of objects from Russia's past.

The Leaning Tower of Pisa

The world-famous tower of Pisa's cathedral began to lean almost as soon as it was built. At almost 197 feet tall and weighing nearly 15,000 tons, perhaps that is not surprising.

The bell tower

Building began on the cathedral's bell tower in 1173. Work was slow because the city of Pisa was so often at war, and it took almost 200 years to complete the tower. The tower began to lean, even before it was complete, because its foundations were too shallow and the earth it is built on is too soft to support its weight. In recent years, thousands of people have climbed to the top of the tower and made the tilt greater. Engineers have used modern technology to reduce the lean slightly but the tower cannot be straightened.

84.5°

The angle

If the tower stood straight, the angle between the tower and the ground would be 90 degrees on each side. Because it leans at an angle of 5.5 degrees, the angle between the tower and the ground is 95.5 degrees on one side and 84.5 degrees on the other.

Galileo Galilei's experiment

Legend says that the scientist Galileo Galilei performed one of his most famous experiments at Pisa. He is said to have dropped two objects of different weights from the top of the tower. Both objects hit the ground at almost the same time. This proved to him that the force of gravity causes everything to fall at the same rate—regardless of its weight.

The bells

To reach the top of the tower where there are seven large bells, you would have to climb 294 stairs—but the bells can be rung from the bottom of the tower using a bell rope.

Pisa Cathedral

Europe

Pisa

ITALY

Mediterranean Sea

DiscoveryFact™

Engineers have been trying to reduce the tower's lean since the Middle Ages.

The Taj Mahal

The Taj Mahal in Agra, India, is a spectacular monument to eternal love. It was built by the Emperor Shah Jahan as a tomb for his favorite wife, Mumtaz.

Building the Taj Mahal

In 1632, Shah Jahan began work on the Taj Mahal. It took 20,000 people 22 years to complete the task. The tomb is reflected in a pool set in the beautiful gardens laid out in front of it. The gardens represent paradise and, like the building, they are perfectly symmetrical.

Did you know?

- The minarets at the corners of the building slope outward slightly. If an earthquake struck the area, the minarets would fall away from the tomb.

- The white marble that covers the Taj Mahal came from a quarry 185 miles away, carried on the backs of 1,000 elephants.

DiscoveryFact™

The marble is cleaned following a recipe that Indian women have used on their skin for centuries. The ingredients include milk and cereal.

Shah Jahan

Shah Jahan planned to build an identical tomb for himself in black marble facing the Taj Mahal. He was overthrown by his son, Aurangzeb, who kept him in prison for the last eight years of his life. To save money Aurangzeb ordered his father to be buried in a tomb beside Mumtaz in the Taj Mahal.

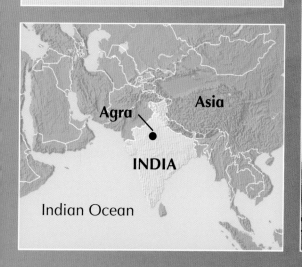

The mosque

There are several other small buildings in the gardens surrounding the Taj Mahal, including memorials to some of Shah Jahan's other wives. One of the most beautiful of these buildings is the mosque, which is made from red sandstone and decorated with marble.

The Great Wall of China

The Great Wall of China is the longest man-made object in the world. It winds for thousands of miles through China, crossing mountains, deserts, and marshland.

Building the wall

In the third century B.C. the Chinese Emperor Qin Shi Huang commanded the construction of a wall to protect his northern border. At this time many walls were already in place, but there were gaps between them that allowed invaders to get through. The emperor linked up these walls to make one Great Wall.

Watchtowers

Watchtowers were built all along the wall. Guards sent messages from one watchtower to the next using smoke signals.

Marching armies

The wall was made wide enough for 10 soldiers to march side by side along the top. Five men on horseback could also ride alongside one another. Today, there are many places where you can still see the wall and you can also walk along it.

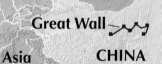

Great Wall

Asia   CHINA   Pacific Ocean

Indian Ocean

The wall today

Some of the oldest sections of the wall have become ruins and have almost disappeared. Other parts, which were built later with stronger materials, have been preserved and some have been reconstructed.

The Easter Island sculptures

The Easter Island heads are among the most mysterious stone statues in the world. We know very little about how they were made and about the people who made them.

The remote island

Easter Island lies in the Pacific Ocean. It is over 1,240 miles from the nearest inhabited island. People first settled on Easter Island about 1,000 years ago. On Easter Day 1722, the island was visited by a European ship and was given the name Easter Island. The people who live there call it Rapa Nui.

Did you know?

- There are over 800 statues on the island. About 230 of these are on platforms along the coast. Many others are unfinished and remain in the quarry.
- The huge sculptures were carved out of rock using stone tools.

The statues

The statues are called "*moai*" by the local people. They sit on stone platforms and some of them face out to sea. Most of the heads are between 13 and 16 feet high but there are some that are nearly twice as tall. Many heads have eyes made from white coral and black stone, and some have hats made from red stone. We do not know why the sculptures were made but they might represent dead ancestors.

How were the statues put in place?

No one is sure how the statues were moved from the place where they were quarried. Local legends say that the statues walked to their platforms. Experts have done experiments to test different ways of moving the stones.

Pacific Ocean

South America

EASTER ISLAND

Atlantic Ocean

Dragging the heads with ropes and using wooden rollers to slide the statues into position were both successful methods. A new idea is that canoes were used as sleds.

The tallest stones are about 33 feet high —that's five times the height of a man.

The Statue of Liberty

One of the most famous landmarks in the United States of America is the Statue of Liberty. It has stood on Liberty Island at the entrance to New York Harbor since 1886.

A gift from France

The statue was a gift from France to America to celebrate 100 years of American independence. The sculptor Frédéric-Auguste Bartholdi created the statue. Inside the statue is an iron frame designed by Gustave Eiffel. There is a small version of the statue in Paris, which is about 30 feet tall.

Did you know?

- The whole structure is 305 feet high from the base of the pedestal to the tip of the torch.
- The Statue of Liberty was used as a lighthouse from 1886 until 1902. The light could be seen for nearly 25 miles.

DiscoveryFact™

The statue was originally built in France and then taken apart, carried on a ship to New York, and reassembled there.

New York State

New York City

UNITED STATES OF AMERICA

Pacific Ocean

Atlantic Ocean

Lady Liberty

The seven rays of Liberty's crown represent freedom spreading out across the world. There are broken chains at her feet, which symbolize freedom from cruel rulers. In one hand she holds a copy of the Declaration of Independence. The torch, which shines in the sunlight, guides people to the "land of the free."

Ellis Island

For many years, immigrants arriving in the U.S. have thought of the Statue of Liberty as a welcome to a new life. Immigrants landed on Ellis Island, near Liberty Island. Here they were given health checks and their details were recorded before they were allowed to go to the mainland. Thousands of people landed here every day until the reception center on the island closed in 1954.

The Declaration of Independence

Liberty carries a tablet in her left hand on which the date July 4, 1776 is written. It was on this date that the United States of America was born, when leaders of 13 American colonies signed the Declaration of Independence. They declared they were independent states, free from rule by Great Britain.

Quick Quiz

Are these sentences TRUE or FALSE?
Place the correct sticker in the box.

1. The leaning tower of Pisa weighs 5,000 tons.
2. The Taj Mahal was built as a tomb for the emperor's wife.
3. The Great Wall of China is 4,000 miles long.
4. The tallest Easter Island statue is 13 feet high.
5. The statue of Liberty was a gift to New York from France.

Find the correct stickers to complete the pictures.

Italy

Russia

India

ANSWERS: 1 – F, 2 – T, 3 – T, 4 – F, 5 – T

Incredible engineering

Engineers are constantly developing new techniques and trying to push the boundaries with incredible designs. In this chapter we look at some of our greatest engineering achievements. Incredible engineering takes you on an amazing journey of discovery, showing you how people have constructed buildings that soar high into the sky, tamed the forces of nature, and even left the Earth to visit new worlds.

The London Eye

The London Eye became the world's largest passenger-carrying wheel when it opened in 2000. On a clear day you can see 25 miles, taking in all the capital's landmarks and the countryside beyond.

The wheel

The London Eye may look like a large bicycle wheel with 80 spokes, but its size presented the designers with problems. A lot of the construction work was done with the wheel lying flat on pontoon bridges in the Thames River. When it was completed, the wheel was lifted upright using cranes.

The Eye has 32 capsules made of curved glass, each of them able to hold up to 25 people. During the ride, passengers can walk around inside the capsule to enjoy the views of London. A round trip is a journey of only about a quarter of a mile, but it lasts 30 minutes. Passengers get on and off while the wheel is moving.

Did you know?

- The London Eye is 443 feet high, almost 130 feet taller than Big Ben, which is nearby.

- The passengers can barely feel the wheel moving. It moves at a speed of one third of a mile per hour.

Atlantic Ocean

UNITED KINGDOM

London •

Europe

Millennium celebrations

The London Eye was built after its designers won a competition for a structure that would celebrate the millennium. It was only intended to stay in place for five years after it opened on December 31, 1999. However, it soon became Britain's most popular visitor attraction, and its future is now guaranteed for at least another 20 years.

Great bridges

Most modern bridges are elegant suspension bridges. They can span enormous distances and are cheaper to build than other types of bridges. Thick cables are stretched between tall towers made from steel or concrete. Smaller cables attached to these hold up the deck of the bridge.

The Golden Gate Bridge

The Golden Gate Bridge across San Francisco Bay is about 1½ miles long and was the world's largest suspension bridge when it opened in 1937. The steel towers that support the two main cables are over 700 feet high. The cables are nearly 3 feet thick, and contain over 25,000 separate wires.

The Akashi-Kaikyo Bridge in Japan is over 2 miles long.

DiscoveryFact™

Suspension bridges look rigid but they are constantly moving. They are designed to cope with high winds and heavy rain, as well as the weight of the traffic.

The Oresund Bridge

Oresund Bridge links two countries, Sweden and Denmark, carrying trains and vehicles across the Oresund Strait. The railroad track runs underneath a four-lane road. The bridge is linked to a tunnel, which carries traffic from Copenhagen, the capital of Denmark, to the Swedish city of Malmö. Oresund Bridge is nearly 5 miles long.

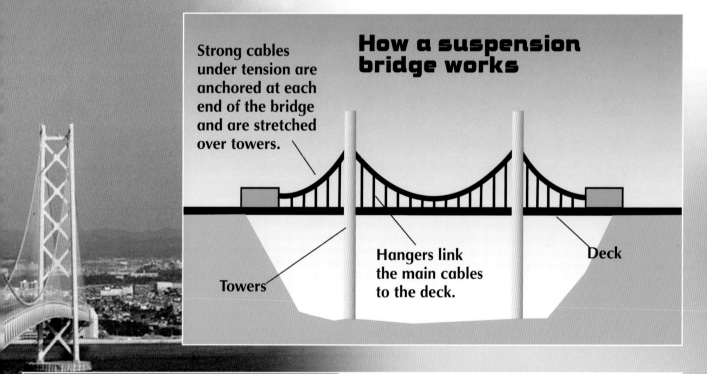

How a suspension bridge works

Strong cables under tension are anchored at each end of the bridge and are stretched over towers.

Hangers link the main cables to the deck.

Deck

Towers

The Millau Bridge

Millau Bridge in France is the world's highest vehicle-carrying bridge. The Tarn River is 886 feet below the deck of the bridge. Seven concrete pylons support the bridge, with 295-foot columns on top of each of them. The tallest column rises 1,125 feet from the floor of the valley, making it higher than the Eiffel Tower.

The Burj Al Arab Hotel

The Burj Al Arab Hotel was designed by Tom Wright to look like an Arab sailboat called a *dhow*. To achieve that, the hotel was built on a man-made island 300 yards off the shore of Dubai in the United Arab Emirates (UAE).

Seven-star hotel

Hotels are usually rated up to a maximum of five stars, though some have given themselves six-star status. Burj Al Arab decided to go one better and call itself the world's only seven-star hotel. The helicopter pad that projects from the building over 500 feet above the ground became the world's highest tennis court when top stars Roger Federer and André Agassi played a match on it.

DiscoveryFact™

The hotel has a seafood restaurant built around a shark-infested aquarium. You have to take a mock submarine ride to reach the restaurant.

Wonderful interiors

The 590-foot-high entrance lobby is the largest in the world. The hotel has just 202 rooms, a lot fewer than most big hotels. That's because each suite is huge. The largest is 8,400 square feet, about the size of three tennis courts. It even has its own movie theater. The hotel is decorated with the finest gold leaf, marble, granite, and crystal.

Asia

Dubai

UNITED ARAB EMIRATES

Arabian Sea

Cooling off

The hotel has luxurious indoor and outdoor swimming pools, and even its own beach.

The CN Tower

The CN Tower in Toronto, Canada, is the tallest free-standing structure in the world. It is 1,815 feet from the ground to the top of the antenna. CN stands for Canadian National, the railroad company that built the tower.

View from the top

The tower has 1,776 steps, the world's longest staircase. Glass-fronted elevators take visitors up the outside of the building in under a minute. At 1,122 feet there is a deck with a glass floor. Above that there is a revolving restaurant, which takes 72 minutes to rotate. Another elevator takes people to the Sky Pod, from where this picture is taken. It is the world's highest observation deck, 1,466 feet above the ground.

Comparing heights

Great Pyramid	Eiffel Tower	Empire State Building	CN Tower
Giza, Egypt	Paris, France	New York, U.S.	Toronto, Canada
452 feet	1,063 feet	1,453 feet	1,815 feet

Did you know?

- The tower was built by pouring concrete into a metal container, like a Jell-O mold. When the concrete set, the container was raised and the process was repeated.

- The glass floor on the 1,122-foot deck is 2½ inches thick and strong enough to take the weight of 14 hippopotamuses.

CANADA

Pacific Ocean

Toronto

North America

DiscoveryFact™

Lightning strikes the tower about 50 times a year on average. The building is protected by copper strips, which conduct the lightning safely down the side of the building to the ground.

The Hoover Dam

The Colorado River regularly flooded the southwestern states of America until the Hoover Dam, named after President Herbert Hoover, was built. The dam stands 725 feet high and was the largest ever built when it was completed in 1935.

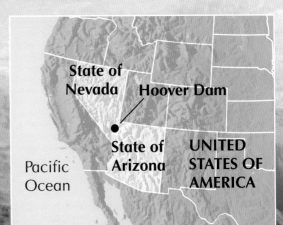

State of Nevada

Hoover Dam

Pacific Ocean

State of Arizona

UNITED STATES OF AMERICA

Powering the south-west

It took 4,000 men four years to build the Hoover Dam. It was built using concrete blocks that were 5 feet high and up to 59 feet long, locked together like a giant Lego set. Water from the dam produces enough electricity for over a million people.

Did you know?

- The Hoover Dam was the first man-made structure to use more building blocks than the Egyptian pyramids.

- The dam lies on the border between Arizona and Nevada, which is marked by a white line. You can stand with each foot in a different state.

Lake Mead

The dam created one of the world's biggest man-made lakes. Lake Mead is over 62 miles long and provides drinking water for about 25 million people. Every year millions of people use the lake for swimming, boating, diving, and fishing. If the water level in the lake rises, it can't go over the top of the dam because there is an overflow, just like in a bathtub or sink. This has happened once, when Lake Mead flooded in 1983.

DiscoveryFact™

The concrete used to build the dam was poured in stages because it produces heat as it sets. If the concrete had been poured all in one go it would have taken 125 years to set.

Quick Quiz

Are these sentences TRUE or FALSE?
Place the correct sticker in the box.

1. The London Eye is almost 130 times taller than Big Ben.
2. The Golden Gate Bridge is found in Manhattan.
3. The Burj Al Arab is the world's only seven-star hotel.
4. The CN Tower is the second tallest free-standing structure in the world.
5. The Hoover Dam used more building blocks than the Egyptian pyramids.

Find the correct stickers to complete this picture of the Burj Al Arab, the world's only seven-star hotel.

ANSWERS: 1−T, 2−F, 3−T, 4−F, 5−T

Index

Index

Acknowledgments

Artwork supplied through the Art Agency by Terry Pastor, Barry Croucher, Robin Carter, and Dave Smith

Photo credits:
b = bottom, t = top, r = right, l = left, c = center

Front cover t Corbis, c Gunter Marx Photography/Corbis, b Jake Wyman/Getty, bl Digital Vision, bc Stephen Studd/Getty, br Corbis
Back cover bl Dreamstime.com
Poster Ronnie Magnusson/Getty

1 Stephen Studd/Getty, 2-3 75 Zena Holloway/zefa/Corbis, 6-7 Micro Discovery/Corbis, 8-9 William Attard Mccarthy/Dreamstime. com, 8cl Anette Linnea Rasmussen/Dreamstime.com, 8cr Dreamstime.com, 9tl Pierre Lahalle/TempSport/Corbis, 10-11 Gabe Palmer/ zefa/Corbis, 10l Dreamstime.com, 11tr Dreamstime.com, 12-13 Visuals Unlimited/Corbis, 13tr Reuters/CORBIS, 14-15 Anthony Redpath/CORBIS, 15tr Mediscan/Corbis, 15bl Dreamstime.com, 16-17 Fendis/zefa/Corbis, 17tr Visuals Unlimited/Corbis, 17bl Anke Van Wyk/Dreamstime.com, 19 Visuals Unlimited/Corbis, 20tc Dreamstime.com, 21bl Bettmann/CORBIS, 22-23 and 23bl Lester V. Bergman/CORBIS, 22cl Lester V. Bergman/CORBIS, 24-25 Duomo/CORBIS, 24bl all Dreamstime.com, 25cr Dreamstime.com, 25bc Dreamstime.com, 26-27 Linda Bucklin/Dreamstime.com, 26 Janet Carr/Dreamstime.com, 27tc Oleg Kozlov/Dreamstime.com, 27cr Rod Ferris/Dreamstime.com, 28-29 Linda Bucklin/Dreamstime.com, 28bl Dreamstime.com, 29tr Jurie Maree/Dreamstime.com, 31 Ben Welsh/zefa/Corbis, 32cl Graça Victoria/Dreamstime.com, 32br Dreamstime.com, 33tr Jaimie Duplass/Dreamstime.com, 33b Katrina Brown/Dreamstime.com, 34-35 Dreamstime.com, 35tr Pete Saloutos/zefa/Corbis, 35br David Badenhorst/Dreamstime. com, 36-37 Najlah Feanny/Corbis, 37tr Lester V. Bergman/CORBIS, 38-39 Robbie Jack/Corbis, 39c Howard Sandler Dreamstime.com, 40-41 Visuals Unlimited/Corbis, 41tr Lester V. Bergman/CORBIS, 43tr Sonya Etchison/Dreamstime.com, 43br Roman Milert/ Dreamstime.com, 45 Visuals Unlimited/Corbis, 46cl Ioana Grecu/Dreamstime.com, 47bl Howard Sochurek/CORBIS, 50tl Tim Pannell/ Corbis, 50-51 Dreamstime.com, 51bl Galina Barskaya/Dreamstime.com, 52-53 Sebastian Kaulitzki/Dreamstime.com, 53tr Dreamstime.com, 53br Wa Li/Dreamstime.com, 54-55 Wa Li/Dreamstime.com, 57 Klaus Hackenberg/zefa/Corbis, 58r Dreamstime.com, 59cr Jason Stitt/Dreamstime.com, 59bc Gert Vrey/Dreamstime.com, 60r Olga Lyubkina/Dreamstime.com, 61tr Dreamstime.com, 61cr Ryan Pike/Dreamstime.com, 61bc Nicolas Nadjar/Dreamstime.com, 62l Linda Bucklin/Dreamstime.com, 62br Paul Moore/Dreamstime.com, 63br Dreamstime.com, 64-65 and 65tl Lester V. Bergman/CORBIS, 65tr Dreamstime.com, 65bl Howard Sochurek/CORBIS, 66-67 Micro Discovery/Corbis, 68-69 Dreamstime.com, 69t Howard Sochurek/CORBIS, 69br Dreamstime.com, 71 Lester V. Bergman/CORBIS, 73tr Ronnie Kaufman/CORBIS, 73cl verett Kennedy Brown/epa/Corbis, 73bc Dreamstime.com, 74 Bob Rowan; Progressive Image/CORBIS, 74cl Dreamstime.com, 75tr Roger Bruce/Dreamstime.com, 75bl Dreamstime.com, 76bl Kamil fazrin Rauf/Dreamstime.com, 77tl Yves Forestier/CORBIS SYGMA, 77cr Richard T. Nowitz/CORBIS, 79tl Doconnell/Dreamstime.com, 79tr Dreamstime.com, 79bl Loke Yek Mang/Dreamstime.com, 80-81 Asther Lau Choon Siew/ Dreamstime.com, 81tl Alistair Scott/Dreamstime.com, 81bl Ilya Gridnev/Dreamstime.com, 83 Visuals Unlimited/Corbis, 84-85 Dreamstime.com, 85tr Dreamstime.com, 86bc Gordana Sermek/Dreamstime.com, 87t Dreamstime.com, 87bl Vladimir Pomortsev/Dreamstime.com, 88bl Daniel Gustavsson/Dreamstime.com, 89br Franz Pfluegl/Dreamstime.com, 90-91 Visuals Unlimited/Corbis, 91br Milan Kopcok/Dreamstime.com, 93tc Dreamstime.com, 93br Yanik Chauvin/Dreamstime.com